Introduction

The Strands

There are four strands in the material:

self-esteem,
communication
relationships.
spiritual and moral development.

The Components

Within these strands fifteen components are addressed, all personal and social skills. These are:

Self-awareness
Building confidence
Developing confidence in speaking
Practising listening
Disclosing feelings
Understanding others
Promoting good relationships
Co-operating with others
Discussing sensitive issues
Promoting a sense of well-being
Developing a sense of belonging
Valuing others
Resolving conflict
Solving problems
Reflection and meditation.

Introduction

Each of the components normally has two, and sometimes three, activities which develop the skills. On the basis of Circle Time being structured once a week there are sufficient activities for a teacher to choose two of these each week from any of the components in order to compile a coherent programme over six years. Please note that the second or third activity under each component is usually the most demanding.

Teachers might want to stay with a strand and component for a period of time or adopt a mixed bag approach. Alternatively teachers might want to stay with a strand for a time but move to other components. An example of the latter approach over two weeks for a Year 3 group is mapped out below.

	Strand	Component	Activity
Week 1	Self-esteem	Self-awareness	a) I'm good at something
	Self-esteem	Building confidence	a) I'm proud of something
Week 2	Self-esteem	Promoting well-being	b) Breathing, calmness
	Self-esteem	Developing a sense of belonging	a) I'm wanted

It is hoped that this resource will inspire schools to explore the use of Circle Time. The intention is that Circle Time will be regarded as a regular, whole school activity and that adults and young people will be committed to the principles.

Record Sheet

6 years of Circle Time

Date	Strand	Component	Activity	Comment

Notes

Self Esteem

Self-awareness
Building confidence
Promoting a sense of well-being
Developing a sense of belonging

Notes

Self Esteem

6 years of Circle Time

✻ Learning Objective

To recognise that each one of us is special and celebrate that.

✻ Activities

1. Someone loves me

Talk about each one of us being special because someone loves us.
Who loves us? - Mummy, Daddy, Granny, Uncle, brother, friend etc.
We all need someone to love us. Think of someone who loves you.
In a round tell us who you think loves you.

2. The mirror game

Place a mirror in a box. All the children are told there is something special in the box. The box is passed around and they all see that it is the children who are special.

3. I like you

Tell the children that we are all special and have different things that we like about each other. In a round the children say something about the child sitting on their right beginning:

"I like _____ because she/he _____ ."

✻ Resources

A cardboard box with a mirror glued to the bottom on the inside.

✱ Learning Objective:

To recognise that everyone is different and to celebrate those differences.

✱ Activities:

1. Same but different

Talk to the children about the ways in which we are the same, and the ways in which we are different.

Ask for some examples of this.

Link up the children in pairs. (If there is not an even number then the teacher joins in to make a pair.)

The children talk in pairs for about one minute with a partner and find two ways in which they are different.

Each member of the pair then feeds back to the whole using the sentence,

"The difference between me and _____ is _____ ."

2. Guess who?

Explain to the children that this is a game about guessing who is being talked about.

Then describe one of the children in the circle giving physical features and personal likes and dislikes (if known) and particular strengths.

The children have to guess who is described.

Whoever guesses continues the game by describing another child.

Self Esteem

6 years of Circle Time

✴ Learning Objective:

To recognise that everyone has a talent and something valuable to offer.

✴ Activities:

1. I'm good at something

Talk to the children about how we are all good at something.
Give an example of what you can do. For example, "I can ... draw."
The children in a round say what they can do, beginning,
"I can _____ ."

2. Guess what I can do

Each child mimes an action of something they are good at, either in or outside school.
The rest of the children try to guess what the mime is and the game continues.
Ask the children to put their hand up before they are invited to answer.

3. Glad you're here

In a round ask the children to say to the person to their right "I'm glad you're in the class because _____" . The idea is that each child affirms the other child's ability to do something. For example "I'm glad you're in the class because you help other people". Or " _____ because you are good at reading".

4. You're okay

Each child has a pen and paper and writes something complimentary about the child sitting on their left. For example, "Sian is a good runner." Then they are collected and read out to the class.

Self Esteem

6 years of Circle Time

* Learning Objective:

To explore one's own feelings and to recognise that other children have feelings which might be different.

* Activities:

1. How are you feeling?

Talk about feelings. We often say "I'm feeling tired, happy, fed up, excited."
Often we show how we are feeling on our faces or with our bodies.
The teacher names a feeling and children have to show the feeling on their faces or with their body. Do this in a round and change the feeling word every few children.

Feeling words: (choose those appropriate to the ability of the children)
Happy; sad; frightened; angry; excited; fed up; surprised; miserable; amazed; bored; shocked; joyful; worried; furious; disappointed; tired; depressed; scared.

2. Name that feeling

Teacher names a feeling and children say the first response that comes to mind. Compile a word list of all the feelings expressed.

3. Musical feelings

Respond to music. Children listen to a variety of musical pieces and they respond by describing how it makes them feel.

4. Picture feelings

Show the children some art work. What feelings do the pictures produce in the children?

* Resources:

Cassette player and suitable music tape.
Pictures/paintings/drawings.

✱ Learning Objectives:

To consider the kind of person I am.

To explore the kind of person I would like to be.

✱ Activities:

1. If I were

In this creative exercise the children are asked to describe themselves using another image. Here they are asked to think of themselves as an animal etc. and explain why they have chosen that particular kind. The statement might come out as a description of a personal characteristic, feelings or wishes.

For example, "If I were an animal I would be a leopard because I am fast".
Other categories might be: car; TV Programme; pop record; TV character; a piece of furniture.

Go on to explore what kind of people the children would like to be using different categories.

2. Who am I?

Talk with the children about who they see themselves to be. For example, are they a son or daughter, a pupil, a sister, brother, niece, nephew, a swimmer, a footballer, a friend etc.?

Divide the children into pairs and ask each child to choose one of the roles you have discussed. The pair share with one another the role chosen and one description of the child in that role. For example, one child might say: "I am a son and I think that I help my parents when I can". In the circle ask for a few examples from the pairs.

✱ Learning Objectives:

To discuss some of the important things in life and discover one's views about these.

✱ Activities:

1. UFO

This activity allows the children to explore their views and values in a number of different areas - their views about the beginnings of life, their priorities in life and their attitude to important relationships.

Divide the class into groups of three. Invite the children to imagine that a UFO had landed and out of it had come one very friendly extra-terrestrial being. "It wants to know all about you. In particular it wants to know how you came into being, what is the most important thing in your life, and why people live together in families. What are you going to say?"

The children discuss this first in their groups. Invite volunteers to give their answers to the questions. They could use the following starting formulae:

I believe we came into being by _____

The most important thing in my life is _____

We live in families because _____

2. Virtual world

Talk with the children about the computer games they have played. Some will be shooting games involving destruction of enemies and aliens; some will be strategy games involving war or building cities or theme parks etc.; some will be adventure and others will be educational. Which ones have they enjoyed?

In this activity the children imagine they are building a new world from scratch. What kind of world will it be? What will be in it? What will they want to leave out from our present world?

In a round each child states one important thing which will be in this new world, and one which will not be in it.

Self Esteem

Building Confidence Year 1

* Learning Objective:

To recognise one's own abilities and achievements.

* Activities:

Before each of these activities the teacher should emphasise that each child is good at something, and that we are now going to talk about what we are good at.

1. What can you do now?

Ask the children to think of something they can do now that they couldn't do when they were younger. They feed this back to the class. For example, "Now I can run fast".

2. What I'm good at

In pairs the children ask each other what they are good at, in and out of school. One example is enough. Each member of the pair feeds back to the whole class what the other said. For example, "Rebecca is good at running".

3. We're all good at something

One child starts off the activity by choosing a member of the group to talk about. For example, "Darren is good at drawing".

Darren then chooses another child and so it continues until everyone is mentioned.

The teacher may need to make sure that each child hears something good about them.

Self Esteem

BUILDING CONFIDENCE | YEAR 2

✱ Learning Objective:

To feel a sense of achievement.

✱ Activities:

Before each of the activities the teacher should discuss how important it is to feel good about ourselves. The activities give examples of how such feelings can be developed and enhanced.

1. Feeling good

Talk to the children about what makes us feel pleased and good about ourselves. In a round ask the children to say what makes them feel good about themselves. For example, "I feel good when I my teacher says I have worked well."

2. Overcoming obstacles

The teacher discusses journeys with children, exploring how they felt when they went on a journey and how they felt when they reached their destination.

The children are asked to close their eyes and the teacher tells the children they are going on an imaginary journey. The teacher talks the children through a particular journey full of obstacles and difficulties:

"You get up late one morning and realise it is Saturday. You have forgotten that you are going to stay with Gran to cheer her up because she is not very well. Your sister helps you with your clothes and breakfast and you are ready on time. Mum takes you on the bus, but as you get on you drop the sweets you are taking for Gran. They are all over the floor. Then the bus leaves and soon you have to get off. What can you do now to make Gran feel better? When you reach her house she answers the door, but does not look very happy. Mum makes her a cup of tea but you feel left out because the sweets are lost.. Gran says "Come and talk to me". When you sit down to talk to her she is really pleased because you are willing to give your time to a lonely old lady. You feel really pleased too that, despite all the things that went wrong, you are able to help her."

Relate these feelings to work in school. Help the children to realise that success is a good feeling.

❋ Learning Objective:

To learn how to set goals.

❋ Activities:

1. Proud of

Children work in pairs and discuss what work they recently have done successfully and are proud of. You might want them to write down the reasons they think it was regarded by the teacher as good work. Each partner then tells the rest of the group what the other was proud of.

2. I want to improve

Children work in pairs and discuss what work they recently have done which was not the best they could do and what they need to improve upon. In a round each child tells the rest of the group how he or she wants to improve. For example, "I want to improve my handwriting".

3. Setting goals

In small groups the children identify how they can improve their work in school and think of ideas on how to achieve their own personal goals. These are then shared with the rest of the class in a round.

For example, "My goal this week is to concentrate better and I am going to achieve it by working quietly and not letting other children disturb me".

As a follow up children could make certificates or badges for a partner and present them during circle time when the goal has been achieved.

Self Esteem

BUILDING CONFIDENCE YEAR 4

6 years of Circle Time

✳ Learning Objective:

To develop skills to resist unwanted peer pressure.

✳ Activities:

1. Resisting pressure

Divide the children into pairs and on a piece of paper give each pair a scenario to discuss. Each scenario requires one child to try to persuade the other to do something and the other child to resist the pressure. Give them a "think time" to prepare what they are going to say and then they carry out the conversation in their pairs. Below are some possible scenarios, but you will want to make some up which are relevant to the group. Make sure that each child gets an opportunity to be put under pressure and practise the skill of resisting that pressure. At the end ask the children how they felt in each of the roles.

- Ride on their bikes through a lonely lane
- Make a swing across a river
- Play with parent's electrical tools in the garage
- Smoke a cigarette
- Pick on one of the children by calling them names.

2. Saying "no"

Divide the children into threes and ask them to think of occasions when it would be important to say "no" - for example, if a friend tries to persuade them to take some sweets from a shop. Each group of three needs to appoint one child to feed back to the whole group the examples they come up with.

Use some of the examples as scenarios for role-play in pairs in which the children practise "saying no". Encourage the children to give a reason for not doing what they are being persuaded to do - for example, "it is too dangerous".

✻ Learning Objective:
To develop skills of decision making.

✻ Activities:

1. Hard decisions

Brainstorm with the whole group the different decisions the children make everyday. For example, what to bring to school as a snack. Discuss who is involved in the decisions and who might be affected - e.g. friends, parents etc.

In a round ask the children to tell everyone a really hard decision they had to make using the words "The hardest decision I had to make was ____".

For example, "....when I had to choose whether I was going to enter the swimming contest". Continue the discussion by asking whether this was the right choice.

Brainstorm a list of examples that involve making decisions. Then identify what risks might be involved - for example health risks (smoking a cigarette); safety risks (playing near a main road).

2. Take Care

Divide the children into groups of three and ask them to make up a code for making safe and sensible decisions. What are the important things to think of? For example, who might be affected, what might be the consequences, what are the risks? Each group feeds back their code in the circle.

You might wish to consider, to help you in your thinking, the TAKE CARE model described here. It sums up all the main considerations when making a choice.

> **C**onsider carefully the situation. Do you know all the facts? Do you need more information.
>
> **A**lternatives need to be looked at. What are the consequences of the different alternatives?
>
> **R**isks should be discussed. If you decide to make that decision what risks are involved? Is it too dangerous?
>
> **E**nd results now must be considered. Are you sure that you are making the right decision?

Self Esteem

6 years of **Circle Time**

BUILDING CONFIDENCE YEAR 6

✱ Learning Objective:

To develop the skill of being assertive.

✱ Activities:

1. Understanding assertiveness

Explain to the children that they are going to learn three new words. These are passive, aggressive and assertive. They are all possible responses to pressure from friends or others. Discuss passive, aggressive and assertive behaviour in order to understand meaning, or, better still, act them out. Use the descriptions below. Ask the children which they think is the best way to act in response to other children putting pressure on them.

> **Passive** - not expressing what you want, feel or believe; letting others take advantage; not standing up for what you believe is right. (Behaviours = being quiet, inactive, timid etc.)
>
> **Aggressive** - always wanting your own way; not caring if you hurt the feelings of others; no respect for others or their wishes. (Behaviours = rudeness, sarcasm, bullying etc.)
>
> **Assertive** - being firm yet respectful; saying what you want but taking into consideration other people's feelings and views; standing up for what you believe is right. (Behaviours = speaking up, making a stand, considering others etc.)

In the circle asks the children simple questions such as "What did you do at playtime?" The children have to respond either passively, aggressively or assertively as you direct them.

2. Being assertive

Write out some situations on cards. There are some ideas below. Children work in groups of three and work out what they might say or do to respond to the situations in a passive, aggressive, and assertive way. These are then fed back to the group in a circle.

> • A friend tries to persuade you to drink some Hooch in the park.
> • Someone in another class continually makes fun of you.
> • Another pupil takes your dinner money.
> • A friend tries to persuade you to sniff a solvent.
> • A friend wants you to bunk off school.

Self Esteem

PROMOTING A SENSE OF WELLBEING YEAR 1

✱ Learning Objective:

To recognise the importance of looking after our own health.

✱ Activities:

1. Keeping healthy

The children jump up and down for a few seconds. Afterwards, they sit quietly and listen to their bodies slowing down . Can they feel their pulse, hear their breathing, feel their heart beating?

Discuss with the children what they could do to keep their bodies healthy.

For example, they could clean their teeth regularly, do some exercise, eat a balanced diet.

In a round ask the children to say one thing they could do to keep healthy.

For example, "To keep healthy I could run every day".

2. Guessing health

In the circle each child is asked to mime an action related to keeping healthy and the rest of the group have to guess what it is. You might want to whisper to each child what it is. Some examples are:

> cleaning teeth; brushing hair; washing face; washing hands;
> having a bath; running; skipping; sleeping; eating fruit.

3. Drawing health

Before Circle Time the children draw a picture of something they need to keep healthy. In the circle each child holds up the picture and says "To be healthy I need _____".

✱ Learning Objective:

To recognise dangers and what is needed to be safe.

✱ Activities:

1. Feeling safe

Ask the children to sit quietly and still. They close their eyes gently and listen to their breathing. Breathe in slowly to the count of four and out slowly. Now ask the children to imagine a time they felt very safe. Where are they? Imagine the sounds/ sights/smells. Who if anyone is with them? Each child in a round describes that time of feeling safe with the words "I feel safe when _____ "

2. The most dangerous place

Talk with the children about dangerous places. What examples can they think of? Then build up with the children an awareness of dangers by creating imaginary dangerous places. For example, "The most dangerous place in the world is a busy road". In a round each child gives a different ending to the sentence - "The most dangerous place in the world is _____."

Ask the children to say, if they can, why their place is so dangerous.

3. Safer schools

How can we make the classroom and the school a safer place?

Divide the class into groups of three and ask each group to come up with some rules for making (a) the classroom and (b) the school, a safer place.

One child from each group feeds back in the circle two rules.

✱ Learning Objective:

To be able to feel calm.

✱ Activities:

1. Circle squeeze

In a circle all the children close eyes. Then, gently but firmly, they take the hands of those on either side of them. Tell the children:

"Imagine that everyone in the circle needs your help and support. Sit quietly for a moment and through your hands send your help and support to everyone (pause). Now think of everyone sending their support to you. See if you can find a good feeling inside which comes from being here with everyone else."

In a round the children say what their feelings were.

2. Breathing calmness

The children sit in a relaxed yet upright stance on their chairs (or on the floor if chairs are not available). Tell the children:

"Sit upright and put your hands, palm downwards, on your stomach so that the tips of the fingers are just touching each other. Begin to breathe slowly and deeply. If you can, breathe in through your nose and out through the mouth. Try to breathe in to the count of four and out to the same number so that your breathing is as slow as possible. Feel your fingers separating and coming together as you breathe deeply. Close your eyes, maintain a steady rhythm and enjoy the peaceful feeling that comes with it."

Ask the children how they are feeling, and when they might use the breathing exercise - for example, when they are feeling upset, worked up, angry etc.

Self Esteem

PROMOTING A SENSE OF WELLBEING YEAR 4

✳ Learning Objective:

To know how to relax and to practise some useful strategies.

✳ Activities:

1. Relax

Explain to the children that there are many ways in which they can calm themselves down and relax when they are feeling upset, angry or have a headache.

What are some of the signs of being upset or worked up, or stressed? (For example, feeling irritated, headache, sweaty palms, fast heart beat etc.).

Offer the following as a strategy the children could use at such stressful times. Say to the children:

"You should be sitting up in a relaxed way but alert and with your back straight. I would like you to imagine that the surface of your feet is covered with tiny, magic holes. (The children may giggle at this but the image appeals to them.) They are usually covered by shutters but you can open them with your mind at any time. Do that now and then, breathing slowly and easily, think of cool air flowing through the holes, up through your legs into your stomach. Hold the air like that for a second and then let it go back down your body and legs, out through the holes, taking all your worries, pains and stress with it."

Ask the children how they feel after the exercise.

2. Musical calm

Play a piece of lively music to the children. Ask them what their feelings were when they were listening. For example, did they feel excited, did they want to dance, etc.?

Then, in contrast, play a quiet, restful piece of music. What did they think of when listening to this? What were their feelings? For example, did they feel calm, relaxed, sleepy etc.?

When might you want/need to listen to quiet, calming music?

✱ Learning Objective:

To develop skills of relaxation.

✱ Activities:

1. Let's relax

Use the script below to introduce a simple exercise involving muscle tension and
relaxation.

*"You need to sit up straight, close your eyes, and concentrate on your breathing. Breathe in and out as
slowly as possible. We are going to think of a number of different parts of the body and relax them.
Let's start with the feet....pretend that you are digging your toes deeply into some sand....hold them
tight in the sand (up to 10 seconds) and then let them go....feel how relaxed your feet are now. Next
lift up your legs and stretch them out in front of you.....feel how tight the muscles are....hold them
there and now place your feet back on the floor....feel how relaxed they are. Now focus on your back.
Arch your back from the chair and hold it there (up to 10 seconds). Sit back in your chair and enjoy
the feeling. We are now going to tighten the neck muscles....stretch your head back and hold....now let
your head fall forward until it is floppy. Hold your hands out with the palms downwards....stretch your
fingers upwards and hold them tight....now relax them.*

*Your body should now feel quite relaxed....breathe in and out slowly....and relax any part of your body
which still feels tense."*

2. Let's fantasise

This guided fantasy is a useful way of relaxing. Use the script below. You might want
to play some quiet music at the same time.

*"You are at the seaside, walking along the sea shore on a warm, sunny day. The sand is damp and
soothing and the sea washes over your feet, cooling them down.*
You stop to sit on a rock. You close your eyes and feel the breeze on your body.
*What sounds do you hear? Perhaps the cry of some seagulls, the waves washing up on to the beach,
some other children playing? You like it here and you are feeling very relaxed and peaceful."*

✱ Resource

The tape "Picture This" by Murray White (1999) provides a
variety of guided imagery exercises.

Self Esteem

PROMOTING A SENSE OF WELLBEING YEAR 6

✻ Learning Objectives:

To understand change and loss.
To share feelings about change and loss.

✻ Activities:

1. All change

Talk to the children about life as a journey. It has a beginning and an end. In between
   lots of important things happen and our lives change. Sometimes the changes are
   enjoyable and exciting; other times they can involve disappointment and even
   unhappiness. Use the analogy of a train. There are stations along the track; sometimes the train goes a different way on a different track.

Individually, before coming into the circle, the children draw the journey of their life.
   The stations are the important changes. They might be starting to walk, first
   teeth, starting school, having a baby brother etc.

In a round invite each child to describe a station (change) in their life and, if they can
   remember, how they felt.

2, Moving on

Talk with the children about the changes that take place in our lives. Sometimes we
   feel a sense of loss when change happens. Ask the children to give examples of
   things that they have lost. It might be a pencil case or a bike or a friend. What
   did they feel like when they lost those things?

Sometimes the changes and losses in our lives are more serious. Divide the group into
   threes and give each group one of the scenarios of loss and change below. They
   should discuss (a) what are the feelings involved, and (b) what can be done. Each
   group feeds back in the circle.

(A useful strategy is RECOGNISE, ACCEPT, WORK THROUGH and MOVE ON.)

- Rebecca has to move house and change school.
- Sally's father moves away and leaves her with her Mum and sister.
- Mohammed's brother dies after a long illness.

✻ Learning Objective:

To recognise a sense of belonging to a family.

✻ Activities:

1. My family

Before Circle Time children draw members of their family. Talk with the children about the importance of families and the different kinds and sizes of families.

In a round the children show their picture and describe who is in their family, using "In my family are _____ ".

2. I like my family

Talk to the children about the good things which come from being in a family. Let them give you the ideas but start them off with, for example, playing with my brother or sister, having a birthday party, not being lonely etc.

In a round the children then complete the sentence: "I like being in my family because _____ ".

31

Self Esteem

DEVELOPING A SENSE OF BELONGING YEAR 2

*Learning Objective:

To begin to develop a sense of belonging to the class.

*Activities:

1. Animals

Give each child the name of an animal from a list of 5 to 8. Call out one or more: "Dogs, (elephants and mice) change places." When you call out "zoo" then everyone changes places.

2. Class rules

What rules do we need to make the classroom a safe and happy place?

Use this time either to establish a set of rules or to consolidate and refine existing ones.

Divide the children into groups of four and ask them to make up the rules they think are important. They should be positive, i.e. begin with "do" as opposed to "don't".

In the circle a representative from each group feeds back the list. From the lists devise the class rules and display them in the classroom.

> **Some Possible Rules**
>
> **Do....**
>
> • Be kind
> • Respect others
> • Listen to others
> • Look after the classroom
> • Work hard

3. You are important to us

Discuss with the children the importance of everyone in the class feeling accepted in the group. Each child has to look around and try to think of something nice about every other child.

The children all stand and one throws a beanbag to another person in the circle. The child who has thrown it must say something complimentary about the receiver of the bean bag starting with "_____ is important to our class because he/she _____".

For example, "Emma is important to this class because she makes people laugh". That person throws the bean bag to another person and continues with the exercise and then sits down. It continues until every one is sitting down.

32

✱ Learning Objectives:

To realise that there are special people who make us feel wanted.
To explore the special places that make us feel secure.

✱ Activities:

1. Wanted

Talk with the children about what we need to make us feel wanted and secure.

Who do we need to make us feel wanted and secure?

Make a list on the board of the suggestions.

In a round the children give one example from the list that they feel is important for them.

For example: I feel wanted when Tracy asks me to play with her.

2. Important

Ask the children to gently close their eyes and relax. They could breathe in (to the count of four) and out (to the count of four) slowly.

When they are relaxed and still ask them to think of a person who is very important to them. Think of their appearance, their voice, their clothes, the things that they do. Think of what they do for you and why they are important. Imagine a day without them. Discuss the children's feelings as a round.

As an additional exercise repeat the procedure for a place. The children think of a place that is special to them. They visualise the colours, the smell, the contents of the place.

✳ Learning Objective:

To develop a sense of belonging to the school.

✳ Activities:

1. The best thing

Talk with the children about the school. What do they like about it? What are the things that they enjoy in school.

In a round the children indicate their feelings about the school with "I belong to _____ school. The best thing about it is _____ ."

2. A better school

Talk with the children about the school. What do they like about it? What is there that could make it a better place? In pairs the children discuss how school could be improved. Ask them to think of two things that should be done to make the school "better". In the circle each child feeds back one suggestion from their discussions.

3. People in school

Discuss with the children who are the people needed to make the school work well.

Brainstorm a list of people, e.g. the secretary, teachers, cook, caretaker etc. Discuss their role and importance.

Prepare some cards with the names of the roles of the people who are needed to make the school work well. Each child picks a school 'job' out of a 'hat' and has to mime that person at work. Once the circle has guessed correctly, discuss why that person is needed.

For example: secretary; headteacher; caretaker; teacher; pupil; lollipop man/woman; dinner lady; cook, etc.

✳ Resources:

Cards with the school "roles" written on.

Self Esteem

✳ Learning Objective:

To develop a sense of belonging to a community.

✳ Activities:

1. My community

Talk with the children about the community in which they live. What are the things
they like about it?

Invite the children to talk about what they appreciate about their neighbourhood
with a round beginning: "I live in _____. The good thing about _____
is_____".

2. Belonging

Discuss with the children how if you are part of a community you normally get involved in some way by joining a club or doing something to help in the community. Before the circle each child prepares on a large sheet of paper a description of
what they do in their community. The children draw a circle in the middle with
"me" in it and then lines out to the different things they do. These might include
swimming club, youth club, church, Brownies, etc.

In the circle each child shows and describes his/her "me and the community" sheet.

3. Help in the community

Discuss with the children who are the people in the community who are a help to us.
They might include police, librarians, youth leaders etc.

In a round each child mentions one person in the community who has been of help to
them with "In the community _____ helped me by _____ ".

Discuss with the children how the community could be improved in some way.
Another round might focus on the help that the children could offer in the community: "I could be of help to the community by _____".

✱ Learning Objective:

To develop and establish a wider sense of belonging.

✱ Activities:

1. Getting to know you

Ask the children to look around the circle carefully. There will be some children who rarely talk to one another and do not know one another very well. Each child tries to meet up with someone they have not talked to for a while and sits with them. They then ask each other three questions:

What do you do in your spare time?

What is your favourite food?

What is your favourite pop group?

In the circle invite any child to share something that they found surprising or interesting in their conversations.

2. Ouch!

Explain to the children that often in a group people will say and do things which cause hurt to others. We shall call these "ouches". Ask the children to give examples of times when they felt an "ouch". Write them on "post-its" or small pieces of paper. The list may well include:

telling tales; being sarcastic; taking others' belongings;
name calling; swearing; bullying.

Discuss what children feel like when these things happen. Explain that in this classroom to make everyone feel welcome and accepted we need to cut out the "ouches". Take the papers with the "ouches" on, ritually tear them up so that the children can see that they are not part of this classroom.

Communication

Developing confidence in speaking
Practising listening
Disclosing feelings

Notes

Communication

DEVELOPING CONFIDENCE IN SPEAKING YEAR 1

✱ Learning Objective:

To be able to introduce oneself and give information about one-self confidently and clearly.

✱ Activities:

These exercises allow children to talk about themselves. They are only examples of what the content could be. The important thing is that they are communicating with the other children, taking turns and making themselves understandable to others.

A useful methodology is to use something that the children can pass around (e.g. a soft toy, bean bag, shell etc.) so that only the child holding the object is allowed to speak. It also provides a focus for the listening behaviour of the others.

I. Greetings

Talk with the children about the times when they might have to tell someone else their name.

Sitting in the circle the children introduce themselves in turn. They should be encouraged to speak clearly and slowly.

"Hello, my name is _____".

2. Favourite food

Talk with the children about the food they eat each day - when do they have it?

Why is it important to eat food? Why is it important to have a healthy diet?

Food usually inspires children to respond in some way.

In a round each child says "The food I like best is _____."

3. Favourite toys

Talk to the children about the toys they have - who gave them? For what occasion? What is their favourite?

In a round each child says "My favourite toy is _____."

Communication

DEVELOPING CONFIDENCE IN SPEAKING YEAR 2

❋ Learning Objective:

To introduce a friend and give information about them
confidently and clearly.

❋ Activities:

1. Introductions

Around the circle each child introduce themselves and the person on the right of
them.

They do this using the phrase: "My name is _____ and this is _____".

This is not only fun, but it does demand concentration and is a good way of introduc-
ing new children into the class.

2. About my partner

In pairs the children find out one thing that the other likes doing.

Around the circle each one of the pair describes what the other likes using the phrase:
"This is _____ and he/she likes _____".

3. We both like

In pairs the children find out two things they both like. They might be swimming,
watching television, playing football etc.

Around the circle each partner tell the whole group one of the things they both like,
using the phrase: "We both like _____".

38

Communication

6 years of Circle Time

DEVELOPING CONFIDENCE IN SPEAKING YEAR 3

✱ Learning Objective:

To be able to describe and talk about someone known and liked.

✱ Activities:

1. Someone I know

Talk with the children about people they "know" well. These could be members of their family, friends, characters from a book you have read with them, or characters from a television programme. They should choose one person.

Allow the children some time then to think of three things to describe their chosen character - e.g. what they look like, what they wear, what they do etc. They can write these down.

In a round the children describe that person to the rest of the group.

2. Someone I like

Talk with the children about people they like. These could be members of their family, friends, people in school, people in the community. Talk about why the children like them. What are the characteristics which make them attractive to the children?

Allow the children some time to think of two things they like about their chosen person. These must be qualities they have. They can write these down.

In a round each child talks about their chosen person to the rest of the group. For example, " I like my cousin because he is kind to me and makes me laugh ."

✱ Learning Objective:

To report on and describe something special.

✱ Activities:

All these activities are opportunities for children to report on and describe special situations. Depending on time and circumstances the descriptions can be more extensive and children should be encouraged to communicate something of the enjoyment and excitement of the situation described.

After the rounds invite the children to ask questions of others if they wish to learn more about their special situation. You might also wish to ask questions.

1. Special times

First talk with the children about enjoyable and special times. Let them briefly give you some examples, and give some yourself. For example, going on holiday, having a pet for Christmas etc.

In the circle each child tells the rest of the group about their special time and why it was special. Begin with the words: "The best time I ever had was when _____ ."

2. Special wish

Talk with the children about the things they would love to have or do if they could have one special wish. Would it be for themselves or for others? Would it be about material things, travel, their family etc.?

When they have had time to think, the children in a round tell the others beginning with the words: "If I had a special wish it would be _____ ."

3. Special person

Talk with the children about the special people in their lives. Let them give you examples. Ask the children to choose one special person apart from their parents.

In a round the children start with: "A really special person in my life is _____ ".

Invite the children to also give the reason why they have chosen that person.

Communication

DEVELOPING CONFIDENCE IN SPEAKING YEAR 5

✱ Learning Objective:

To express opinions about a wide range of issues.

✱ Activities:

All these exercises are about the importance of forming our own views about different issues and not being afraid to say what we believe. It is useful to allow the children to discuss these in small groups first when they will be able to hear other opinions. Then in the circle they can communicate their own view.

1. My views about school

Allow the children to discuss the topics in small groups of three or four and then they give their opinion in a round in the circle. This exercise suggests statements about school and the children have to decide after discussion whether they agree or disagree. They must then give a reason.

Examples of statements:

- Homework is a good idea for all pupils
- School uniform should be optional
- School holidays should be shorter
- Pupils who misbehave badly should be punished
- Pupils should be able to choose which subjects they study.

2. My opinions

Allow the children to discuss the issues in small groups of three or four and then they give their opinion in a round in the circle. This exercise suggests statements about life and moral issues in general and the children have to decide after discussion whether they agree or disagree. They must then give a reason.

Examples of statements:

- People who murder should be put to death
- Smoking should be banned in public
- Children should be allowed to stay up as long as they want
- The violence shown on TV and videos is harmful
- Nuclear weapons should be banned.

✳ Learning Objective:

To become more competent in using spoken language.

✳ Activities:

1. Brilliant Ben

Allow the children some time in pairs to think of an alliterative adjective/verb to match their name, e.g. 'Brilliant' Ben, Ben is bowling'. It need not make too much sense and this will be a fun activity.

In the circle they then use the ideas they came up with. For example:

> My name is brilliant Ben.
> Today Ben is bowling.

2. Who's on the telephone?

Talk with the children about who might make a telephone call to their home.

Examples might be: a friend; a relative; telephone sales person; the optician; the dentist etc.

In the circle the children pass round a toy telephone and make up a response to an imaginary call. The rest of the children have to guess who it was they were talking to.

Communication

6 years of Circle Time

✱ Learning Objective:

To listen carefully and respond appropriately.

✱ Activities:

Explain to the children how important it is to listen carefully when someone else is talking. Ask them what might happen if they did not listen to other people. For example, they might do the wrong thing, or go to the wrong place etc.

1. How do you do?

In the circle each child calls out the name of the next child to their right. On hearing their name that child responds with a smile.

Alternatives might be a handshake, saying "hello", etc.

2. That's me!

Sitting in the circle the children listen as the teachers calls out their date of birth. They respond in the way you have agreed - e.g. by jumping up, cheering, clapping etc.

3. Stand up and turn around

The teacher shouts out certain reasons for standing up and turning around. Make them up on the basis of your knowledge of the children and on what they are wearing. Here are some examples: "Stand up and turn around if......"

..you are wearing trainers

..you had cereal for breakfast

..you are wearing something red

..you like this school

..you are happy

..you are sad at the moment.

Note: If you move on to more serious statements such as the last one, you need then to allow pupils to share their feelings and be ready to follow this up either in the whole group or on a one to one basis.

✱ Learning Objective:

To listen carefully and respond appropriately.

✱ Activities:

Explain to the children how important it is to listen carefully when someone else is talking. Ask them what might happen if they did not listen to other people. For example, they might do the wrong thing, or go to the wrong place etc.

1. Musical messages

Choose three musical instruments (e.g. maracas, bells, tambourine). Show them to the children and let them hear what they sound like.

Then decide for each instrument the response you want from the children. For example when you play the bells, they all stand up and turn around; the tambourine = all clap hands; the maracas means all dance.

In the circle the children close their eyes, or sit facing outwards. The teacher makes the musical sound and the children listen carefully and respond accordingly.

2. Simon Says

Play the traditional "Simon Says" game. It demands careful listening and concentration.

Communication

6 years of Circle Time

✱ Learning Objective:

To listen with concentration.

✱ Activities:

1. Sounds

Start with a relaxation exercise with the children by asking them to close their eyes gently, and then breathe in and out slowly, to the count of four if they can. Ask them if they are feeling relaxed.

Then ask the children to listen to the sounds they can hear outside the room. Allow them to do this for about half a minute. Invite the children to say what they heard.

Repeat the procedure, but this time ask them to listen to the sounds inside the room.

Finally, repeat the procedure and ask them to listen to the sounds within their bodies - for example, you might get breathing, gurgling, beating of the heart etc.

2. Got it taped

Prepare a tape of sounds and play it to the children. How many can they recognise?

3. Musical pictures

Play some different pieces of music. Allow the children to listen and invite them to describe to the rest of the group the pictures that came into their mind.

Communication

PRACTISING LISTENING YEAR 4

6 years of Circle Time

✱ Learning Objectives:

To listen carefully and develop short term memory.

✱ Activities:

1. For my birthday

Teacher starts the round by saying "For my birthday I had a game." The next child repeats that and adds one more, and so it goes on. See how far you can get around the circle in the same way. When it gets impossible start again.

Using the same procedure start with "I went shopping and bought some tomatoes."

Use the same procedure and start with "I went to the zoo and saw an elephant."

2. Meet my partner

Divide the class into pairs and give each pair a few minutes to question one another.

Choose three questions from the list below or make up your own.

What is your middle name?

What did you have for breakfast?

What is your favourite song?

What job would you like to do when you are older?

If you could choose any birthday present what would it be?

If you could travel to anywhere in the world where would it be?

Each child now introduces his/her partner to the rest of the group giving the responses to the three questions.

For example: This is Mandy. Her middle name is Elizabeth, she had cornflakes for breakfast and she would like to visit Orlando.

Communication

6 years of Circle Time

✱ Learning Objective:

To realise the importance of listening carefully.

✱ Activities:

1. The magic box

Provide a "magic box" in which is a sufficient number of cards for each child to pick out one. On each card is the name of an object. In turn each child picks out a card and tells the group two things about the object. For example, if it is an orange the child could say "It is round and you can eat it". The rest of the children try to guess what it is.

2. Favourites

Divide the group into pairs and allow a fixed amount of time for each partner to tell the other a few facts about their favourite TV character.

The other partner can ask any questions to clarify anything. Allow about half a minute for each.

In a round each child tells the rest of the group what their partner had told them.

Repeat the above procedure but explore favourite food, favourite games, favourite characters in a story, etc.

✱ Learning Objective:

To listen carefully to another person's experiences.

✱ Activities:

1. What a day

In pairs the children tell each other about the best day they have ever had. Each pair then joins up with another pair and each of the children in the group of four tells the others in the group about their partner's best day.

The procedure could be repeated with their best journey, best present, best holiday, best piece of work in school, etc.

It is also possible to ask each child to feed back in a round: "The best day I ever had".

2. Are you listening?

Talk with the children about the effect that you can have on other people when they are talking to you and you are not listening. How might it feel? Explain that we are now going to try it out.

Divide the group into pairs and each pair decides who is A and B. A tells B about his/her hobbies or leisure activities. B tries not to listen. What did the non-listeners do? For example, looks away, yawns, looks out of the window, sighs etc. How did A feel?

Now B tells A about his/her hobbies and leisure activities. A listens well. What did A do? For example, made eye contact, nodded now and again, showed interest etc.

Talk about how important it is to use our bodies when we are listening. Not only does it help us concentrate but it shows respect to the other person.

Communication

DISCLOSING FEELINGS YEAR 1

✱ Learning Objectives:

To be able to discuss the feelings of the three baby owls.

To be able to express how we feel at certain times.

To understand ways in which we can help one another when we are feeling unhappy.

✱ Activities:

1. Owl talk

Talk with the children about how stories give us lots of different feelings and that it is good to talk about our feelings.

Divide the class into pairs and ask them to tell each other how they are feeling. They can use the starter: "Today I am feeling _____ ."

Give an example yourself, such as "Today I am feeling pleased".

Each child then in a round tells the rest of the group how they are feeling today.

In the same pairs the children then discuss how they think the baby owls were feeling when they discovered one night that Mummy had gone.

They can use the starter: "When the baby owls found that their Mummy had gone they felt _____."

Each child then in a round tells the rest of the group their statement.

2. "I want my Mummy"

Talk with the children about how the baby owls were missing their Mummy and were feeling all the things that they had already described in the previous activity.

Invite the children in pairs to tell one another of a time when they felt lonely or afraid.

What can we do to help other children when they feel lonely or afraid? Sarah the baby owl got them to cuddle up on her branch. Ask the children to discuss that in pairs and then in a round to complete the sentence: "When someone is lonely or afraid we can help by _____ ".

✱ Resources:

"Owl Babies" by Martin Waddell (1994) Walker Books.

Communication

6 years of **Circle Time**

❋ Learning Objective:

To recognise that feelings can be revealed through facial expressions.

❋ Activities:

1. You look happy

Talk with the children about "feelings" words. Give an example ("pleased") and ask the children to provide other examples. Make a list of them on the board or where they can be seen.

In the circle each child looks to his/her left and makes a statement about how the child looks today, using a feeling word from the list - for example, "Jason, you look pleased today". Jason then has to show his pleasure on his face, and also using his body. Continue around the circle.

2. Guess what?

Talk with the children about "feelings" words. Give some examples, and invite some from the children. Write the list where the children can see them. Each child chooses one feelings word without disclosing it to anyone else.

In the circle each child mimes a feeling and whoever is sitting on the left tries to guess the feeling. If he/she cannot then the rest of the group is invited to guess.

Communication

DISCLOSING FEELINGS YEAR 3

Learning Objectives:

To recognise how feelings can be revealed through body language.

✱ Activities:

Talk with the children about how we show our feelings with our bodies. Give some obvious examples and let the children together, led by the teacher, make some really exaggerated body poses to represent - anger (tearing the hair), fear (eyes and mouth open) and delight (big smile and arms open wide).

1. Miming feelings

Divide the class into groups of three. Give each group a card on which is a feeling word. Allow each group a short amount of time to organise themselves until they are ready to mime that feeling in front of the class. The rest of the children try to guess the feeling.

Examples of feeling words for the mime: worried; miserable; embarrassed; glad; joyful; scared; helpless; nervous; excited.

2. Statue feelings

The children work in pairs. Each pair is given a card on which are written some feeling words. The children then adopt a statue pose which represents the feeling or emotion. The rest of the children try to guess the word.

✱ Resources:

Cards on which are printed the "feeling" words.

Note: For an extensive list of feeling cards, illustrated with a cartoon picture, see Circle Time Resources by George Robinson and Barbara Maines, (1998) available from Lucky Duck Publishing.

6 years of Circle Time

✱ Learning Objective:

To recognise how feelings can be revealed through tone of voice.

✱ Activities:

Talk with the children about how our voices show what we are feeling. Give some obvious examples and allow the children together to try them out. For example, all say "I can't find my exercise book" in an excited way, a frightened way, a couldn't care less way.

1. It's good to talk

Use a toy telephone which is passed around the circle from child to child. Each child picks out a feeling card from a collection which you have previously prepared. As they speak into the 'telephone' each child says: "Hello, how are you" - conveying the emotion or feeling through tone of voice only. The child on the left has to guess what it is and reply "Hello, you sound _____ today."

2. My feelings

Each child picks out a "feeling" word from a collection you have previously prepared. In a round they use the card to make a statement about their own feelings at a particular time. Each begins with: "I get really _____ when _____ ."

Suggested Words: :

irritable;	worried;	depressed;	miserable;	embarrassed;
nervous;	scared;	helpless;	tired;	upset.
glad;	joyful;	excited;	pleased;	proud;
delighted;	curious;	interested;	happy:	confident.

✱ Resources:

Toy telephone.
Cards on which are printed the "feeling" words.

Communication

6 years of Circle Time

DISCLOSING FEELINGS YEAR 5

✱ Learning Objective:
To explore feelings in imaginative and creative ways.

✱ Activities:

It is recommended that before each of these activities you allow the children to have some time for preparation. However, if a child is stuck during the round, but does not want to "pass", then the other children can join in to help him/her.

1. Colourful language
Talk with the children how colours are often linked to different feelings or emotions - e.g. grey and downcast, blue moods, green with envy etc. Each child chooses a colour and uses it describe how he/she is actually feeling or as an example of feelings. For example: "I am feeling like red because I am angry."

2. Fun with names
The children in a round have to find a way of describing themselves and their feelings using the same letter as their first names. This is a fun activity and the descriptions will not necessarily be valid.
For example, "My name is Anne and I am feeling awful."
   "My name is Brian and I am feeling brilliant."

3. If I were _____ .
In this creative exercise the children are asked to describe themselves as an animal etc. and explain why they have chosen that particular example. The statement might come out as a description of a personal characteristic, feelings or wishes.
For example, "If I were an animal I would be a leopard because I am fast."

Other categories might be:
fruit;	TV Programme;	pop record;
car;	TV character;	a piece of furniture.

Communication

DISCLOSING FEELINGS YEAR 6

✱ Learning Objective:

To discuss strong feelings and share concerns and worries.

✱ Activities:

1. Strong feelings

This is an opportunity for pupils to share their feelings about current issues. Divide the children into small groups to discuss the issues first. Then as a result of their discussions they articulate their feelings beginning with: "When I think about _____ I feel _____." Use ideas which are topical and relevant, but the ideas below might help.

Possible topics for discussion: bullies; drugs; getting drunk; school rules; times set for going to bed; violent videos.

2. Sharing feelings

Talk with the children about times when we hide our feelings. Is this a good thing? This is an opportunity for pupils to talk about disappointments and worries with the group (e.g. they might include not being chosen for a team, hospital appointments etc.) It might also include loss (e.g. losing a friend, a pet dying). It can only be done in a supportive and trusting environment. After the round talk about how the group can help those children who have shared their disappointments.

The round might begin with either "I am worried about _____" or "I am really disappointed at _____".

Relationships

Understanding others
Promoting good relationships
Co-operating with others
Valuing others
Resolving conflict

Notes

Relationships

6 years of **Circle Time**

✳ Learning Objective:

To learn about what the other children enjoy.

✳ Activities:

1. Best presents

Talk with the children about how we are different and how we like different things. It is important to understand one another and this activity is one way we are going to learn a little about one another.

Wrap up a box as a special present. The children pass it around the circle and tell the others about a special present. Use the words: "The best present I ever had was ____."

2. Home is where

Talk with the children about how we are different and how we like different things. It is important to understand one another and this activity is one way we are going to learn a little about one another.

Ask the children to think about what they really like doing at home. In a round they tell the other children about this.

Use the words: "When I'm in my house I like_____."

✳ Resources:

A box wrapped up in an attractive way as a present.

Relationships

UNDERSTANDING OTHERS   YEAR 2

❋ Learning Objective:

To understand what makes children in the group happy and sad.

❋ Activities:

1. What makes you happy?

Talk with the children about the importance of understanding other children and looking for ways in which we can understand them better. Ask the children for examples of what has made them happy recently.

Divide the group into pairs. Each pair must agree on one thing that makes them both happy. One of the pair feeds back in a round.

For example, We are both happy when we go out to the park.

2. What makes you sad?

Talk with the children about the importance of understanding other children and looking for ways in which we can understand them better.

Each child writes on a card one thing that has made them sad. These are placed in a box and each child takes out one and reads it to the group. The teacher asks for ideas about how the group could help someone feeling that way.

❋ Resources:

Cards for the "What makes you sad" activity.

Relationships

6 years of Circle Time

✱ Learning Objective:

To understand how other children think of themselves

✱ Activities:

1. Either/or

Explain to the children that this is a fun activity which will also help us to understand one another a little more.

Divide the group into pairs and give each pair a card with some pairs of words on. The children decide which they would prefer to be and why.

In the circle read out examples of the pairs and ask for volunteers to say their choice and why. Here are some examples:

Would you like to be...

A tree or a flower	A ship or a plane	Rich or healthy
Happy or handsome	A monkey or a lion	Young or old
Boy or a girl	Pop star or teacher	Athlete or musician.

2. My badge

Before the circle ask the children to draw a badge which represents themselves in different ways. Divide the badge into three parts and in each the children draw something that represents some aspect of their life.

> In one part will be something that they can do.
> In the second will be something that they would like to do.
> In the third part will be a word or phrase which sums them up.

In the circle each child describes his/her badge.

✱ Learning Objective:

To learn about how other children can feel during a day in school.

✱ Activities:

1/5/03

1. Weathering the day ✓

Talk with the group about a typical school day. What are the high points and what are the low points? Ask for some examples from the children.

In a round invite the children to identify what are for them the high and low spots and what they are feeling at those times. Use the symbolism of sunny intervals and cloudy spells.

For example: "A sunny interval is when we have Circle Time - I feel refreshed. A cloudy spell is when I can't do my maths - I feel depressed."

✓ 1/5/03

2. Target practice

Talk about the times in the school day when we are "off target". That might mean we lose concentration, don't work as hard as we can, don't feel very interested, don't enjoy what we are doing. Invite the children to give examples of such times.

Discuss how we can get back on target and try to improve our performance. In a round the children share when they are "off target" and need to get back "on target".

For example: "I need to get back on target by concentrating better when I am listening to the teacher".

Relationships

UNDERSTANDING OTHERS   YEAR 5

✱ Learning Objectives:

To understand what makes other children feel up or down.

To consider ways to help those when they are "down".

✱ Activities:

1. Titanic

Talk with the group about what gives them that "sinking feeling". This is when things go wrong and may be something related to school or at home or in their relationships with friends. Ask the children for examples of recent "sinking feelings".

In a round each child talks about a time when things went wrong, and what happened to put it right, or what he/she would have like to have happened.

For example, "I had a sinking feeling when I lost my dinner money. My Mum brought some more."

2. Concorde

Talk with the group about the times when they felt they were "flying high".

This is when things are going really well and may be something related to school or at home or in their relationships with friends. Ask the children for examples of recent "flying high" feelings.

In a round each child tells of a time when things were going really well.

For example, "I was flying high when I won my heat on sports day."

6 years of Circle Time

✱ Learning Objectives:

To understand how others might react in certain situations.
To explore other children's values.

✱ Activities:

1. Value Added

Introduce the subject by explaining that the way we respond to different situations
    reflects our values, i.e. what we believe to be important in life.

The activity attempts to dig out values.

Divide the group into threes and give them a card on which is written one scenario.
    The children decide (a) what they would do, and (b) what the values are that are
    being addressed. For example it might be honesty, respect for others, loyalty to
    friends, etc.

Examples of scenarios:

Mandy / Chloe
- Two children find a bag in the park. It looks old and battered. When they look inside there is a twenty pound note and a library card with a name and address on it.

Natalie / Jasmin
John / Jake
- You are with your friend when one of them brings out some chocolate bars. He says he stole them from the newsagents, and offers them round.
- You are on the bus and some of your friends start to make fun of an old man sitting at the front. He is dirty and smelly and seems homeless.

Joe
- You have arranged to go to the cinema with two of your friends. The night before, another friend rings up and says that her family are offering to take you away for the day to an amusement park.

Jessica
- You are out with your friends and one of them asks an older teenager to get some alcoholic drinks from the off-licence. They want you to go into the park to drink the cans.

60

✱ Learning Objective:

To discuss what it means to welcome new members of the class and to be caring towards everyone.

✱ Activities:

1. Welcome Teddy

Talk with the children about the importance of treating one another properly in the classroom. What if a child was new to the class? What might he/she be feeling like?

Using a teddy bear to pass around the circle the children say what they would do to make him/her feel welcome as a newcomer to the class.

2. Cheer up everyone

What if someone was unhappy today in the class? What could we say to cheer him/her up?

Pass around the teddy and invite each child to make a "cheering up" statement.

3. Cheer up, teacher

What if the teacher was feeling a bit under the weather? What could we say to cheer her/him up? In the circle the children respond by suggesting what they would say to or do for the teacher who needs cheering up.

Relationships

PROMOTING GOOD RELATIONSHIPS YEAR 2

6 years of Circle Time

✱ Learning Objective:

To learn about the nature of friendship and to discuss what it means to have a good friend and be a good friend.

✱ Activities:

1. Having a friend

Talk with the children about friendship. What is the purpose of friendship and what makes a good friend. Brainstorm "what makes a good friend" and write up some of the ideas.

In a round the children say what they think a good friend is like, starting with the phrase: "A good friend is someone who _____".

2. A gift of friendship

Talk with the children about the importance of "being a friend" as well as "having a friend". Being a friend means that we have to give something of ourselves to our friends, e.g. time, help, etc. We all need to be good friends to one another in the class. Brainstorm a list of things that we could give to others to show we are good friends.

The children pass around a bowl to one another. On the bowl is a "gift of friendship", one of the ideas from the brainstorm. Use the words: "My gift of friendship to you is _____."

✱ Resources:

A wooden bowl for the "gifts of friendship".

Relationships

PROMOTING GOOD RELATIONSHIPS YEAR 3

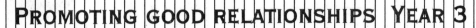

✱ Learning Outcomes:

To discuss ways of being kind at home and at school.

✱ Activities: *done -3/7/03*

1. Home and away

Talk with the children about good relationships in school and at home. What do we feel like when relationships are bad? What do we feel like when relationships are good?

Produce beforehand an outline of a school and a house. The children write down on a "post-it" one thing they will do to be kind to people at home, and on another one thing they will do to be kind to people in school. The "post-its" are put onto the drawings.

In the circle the children start with: "At home I will _____" and "In school I will _____."

2. Happy families

Ask the children to bring in beforehand a photograph of themselves with a member or members of their family.

In the circle each child chooses one of the people in the photograph with whom they get on really well and explain why.

Use these words: "I get on really well with _____ because _____ _____ ."

Discuss at the end the reasons given and analyse how they can promote good relationships.

✱ Resources:

Post-its.
Drawings of the school and house outlines.

63

Relationships

PROMOTING GOOD RELATIONSHIPS   YEAR 4

6 years of Circle Time

✱ Learning Objective:
To understand how we can build a good relationship with the local community.

✱ Activities:

1. Welcome
Who are the important people in the community? Brainstorm a list.

This might include firefighters, nurses, shopkeepers, police etc.

How can bad relationships arise between us and these people (e.g. rudeness, shoplifting, etc.)? How can good relationships be made?

Invite a member of the community into a Circle Time session. Prepare for the visit by working out questions to ask, and how the group will make the visitor welcome.

2. Invasion
Explain to the children that this is an imaginary exercise to help us think about our community and the ways that we can make it a better place to live in.

"We have just been invaded by some friendly aliens. They look around and see the mess in our community. For example, litter around the streets, cars polluting the air etc. They give us two wishes. They will change anything we want. Talk in pairs for two minutes and come up with two wishes for the aliens to make our community a better place."

In a round each pair tells the others the two wishes they have agreed upon.

Relationships

✱ Learning Objective:

To begin to understand some ways in which good relationships can be developed in society and the world.

✱ Activities

1. What's wrong with the world?

Ask the children to bring in newspaper cuttings about problems in society and in the world. Talk with the children about these and make a list of them. It might include crime, unemployment, violence, war etc.

In the circle the children are asked how some of these problems might be resolved. Use the words: "If I were the government I would _____ ."

2. Star Wars

Explain to the children that this is an imaginary exercise to help us think about our world and how to make it a better place to live in.

"There is a battle going on between the forces of light and the forces of darkness. The forces of light have some interesting new weapons and they can be used to change the world. If you had control of these magic weapons how would you use them?"

Discuss in threes what you would do with the three weapons to bring about better relationships and a better way of life.

The weapons are:

- The health ray - this will cure one disease only.
- The laser transformer - this will change any substance to another of your choice.
- The moral detonator - this will explode any evil of which you wish to rid the world.

Each child feeds back from the groups how they would use one of the weapons.

Relationships

PROMOTING GOOD RELATIONSHIPS YEAR 6

6 years of **Circle Time**

❋ Learning Objective:

To discuss ways of supporting friends when they are in difficulties.

❋ Activities:

1. Turn around

Talk with the children about how friends sometimes can do things which you think are wrong (e.g. lying, being unkind, poor attitude in class). Divide the class into small groups and ask them to brainstorm a list without mentioning the actual friends.

Write the listed behaviours on pieces of paper and put them in a container. Repeat some of them in order that there are sufficient - one for each pair. Each pair discusses a behaviour and comes up with two suggestions of what should be done to "turn around" the friend. Each child in the pair feeds back one of them in the circle.

2. Problems

What would you do to help a friend who had told you a "secret" about themselves. For example, the friend had a big problem, such as being bullied or was unhappy at home. What would you do to help? Divide the class into pairs to discuss the problems and come up with some advice.

Feedback the advice in the circle.

Some possible secrets:
- Some pupils are stealing your friend's money
- Your friend is sniffing solvents
- Your friend is staying out all night
- Your friend is skipping some lessons.

Relationships

CO-OPERATING WITH OTHERS   YEAR 1

6 years of **Circle Time**

❋ Learning Objective:

To feel a sense of togetherness.

❋ Activities:

1. Pass it on

These are fun activities but also emphasise the corporate nature of the group. Something has to be passed on from person to person yet the whole group is affected.

The following things could be passed around the circle:

Children hold hands and pass a squeeze; a Mexican wave with hands; a Mexican wave by standing and sitting; a smile; a wink; shaking hands; a nod.

2. Here it comes

In this activity different sounds are passed around.

They could be the sounds of:

a car; a motorbike; a plane; a police siren; a hum.

To make it more challenging arrange a given cue for the sound to be passed around in the opposite direction - for example when you shout "change direction".

Relationships

CO-OPERATING WITH OTHERS   YEAR 2

❋ Learning Objectives:

To understand the feelings of those who need help but who do not receive it.

To identify ways to be helpful to others in the group.

❋ Activities:

1. Change places

This is a fun game which can be used as an "ice-breaker" or "energiser". Here, however, it leads on to more serious discussion about the importance of good relationships, helping and co-operating with others.

The teacher says "Change places if _____." and adds different endings. They start with fun endings and can become more serious. Here are some ideas.

Change places: if you have a pet; if you are wearing something blue; if you had toast for breakfast; if you can swim; if you like Manchester United etc.

When they get the hang of it, invite the children to make up some categories.

The teacher leads on the final one: Change places if you have been helped by someone recently. Invite the children to talk about how it felt being helped by someone.

Refer to the story of The Little Red Hen and ask the children in pairs to discuss how they think she felt when no-one was willing to help her using some feeling words.

2. Better things to do

Talk with the children about how the animals, when they were asked to help the hen, said that they had better things to do. Encourage the children to think of occasions when they were asked to help someone. Invite them to talk about those occasions and how the other person would have felt if they had said, "I've got better things to do"?

Discuss with the children the importance of being helpful to others in the class.

Each child is given a card on which they complete the sentence starter: "I can be more helpful to others in this class by _____ _____ ." In a round they read it out to the whole class.

❋ Resources:

The story of The Little Red Hen. (Traditional tale.)

Cards on which to write the sentences.

Relationships

CO-OPERATING WITH OTHERS   YEAR 3

6 years of **Circle Time**

Learning Objective:

To work with others in a co-operative way.

* Activities:

1. Getting it together

This is a fun game but is also an excellent co-operative activity. Divide the children
into groups of three or four. Prepare beforehand some cards on which are written
the names of objects. Each group must mime the object, which may well have
some moving parts. Each member of the group must be involved.

The other group have to guess what the object is.

Examples of the objects are:

a car; bridge; washing machine; lawn mower; kettle; piano.

2. Just the job

Divide the children into threes. Prepare beforehand some cards on which are written
the names of occupations.

Each group has to perform a mime which demonstrates the occupation and the other
groups have to guess what it is.

Examples of the occupations:

newspaper reporter; teacher; bus driver; doctor; dinner lady;
postman; dentist; shopkeeper; fireman; secretary; car mechanic;
supermarket checkout assistant.

* Resources:

Cards on which are written objects for miming.
Cards on which are written occupations for miming.

Relationships

6 years of Circle Time

❋ Learning Objective:

To discuss ways in which we can be helpful and not hurtful.

❋ Activities:

1. Hedgehogs

Talk with the children about how we can be prickly like hedgehogs i.e. we can hurt others by what we say or do.

In pairs the children think of two ways in which it is possible to be a hedgehog at home with brothers and sisters or mums and dads.

In the circle each member of the pair gives one example. Pass around something prickly as each child takes part.

Children use the phrase: I can be a hedgehog by _____ .

Repeat the process by discussing how it is possible to be a hedgehog in school.

2. Cushions

Talk with the children about being like cushions, which are soft and comfortable to the body. We can be like cushions to others i.e. caring and nice to be with.

In pairs the children think of two ways in which it is possible to be a cushion at home with brothers and sisters or mums and dads.

In the circle each member of the pair gives one example. Children use the phrase: "I can be a cushion by _____." Pass around a cushion as each child takes part.

Repeat the process by discussing how it is possible to be a cushion in school.

Relationships

6 years of Circle Time

* Learning Objective:

To develop the skills necessary for working together.

* Activities:

1. Tall towers

Divide the class into groups of three. Give each group two paper cups, some paper clips, three pieces of newspaper. The challenge is to build the tallest tower they can in four minutes.

Judge the competition and then ask representatives from the groups how they came to build their tower. In what way did they work together?

2. Let's work it out

The following scenarios are to be used for small groups to consider and co-operate in attempting to decide upon a solution. The children need to give their reasons for their decision.

A UFO lands in the park. There is no one around apart from you and your friend. An alien steps out of the space craft. It extends its arms to you. What do you do?
  - (a) Run away and hide   (b) Tell someone
  - (c) Walk up and greet it   (d) Phone the police   (e) Other suggestions.

You find an injured dog by the side of the road. What do you do?
  - (a) Ignore it - there's nothing you can do (b) Pick it up and cuddle it
  - (c) Bandage up its wounds   (d) Tell someone
  - (e) Other suggestions.

You are with your friend and you find some drugs on the pavement. What do you do?
  - (a) Take them home   (b) Leave them there   (c) Inform the police
  - (d) Show them to some other friends   (e) Other suggestions.

* Resources:

Materials for building the tower - newspapers, paper clips, plastic cups.

Relationships

6 years of **Circle Time**

✱ Learning Objective:

To work together to achieve a common goal and a common experience.

✱ Activities:

1. Cool rhythm

In the circle start a rhythm going by using both hands and slapping your thighs twice followed by clicking the fingers twice. When you are ready, at the same time as you click your fingers the second time you call out one of the children's names. He or she also joins you in the rhythm and when ready calls out another name. This goes on until all the children are named and everyone is joining in the rhythm.

2. Together

Talk with the children about working together and co-operating. What are the advantages of co-operating? What are the consequences of not co-operating?

Introduce a symbol of co-operation - for example, a chain. Pass it around the circle. What does the chain say about co-operation? Use some other examples - a circular object; a ring; a family.

Divide the group into pairs and ask the children to think of some other symbols of co-operation.

Relationships

VALUING OTHERS   YEAR 1

✳ Learning Objectives:

To appreciate the importance of being kind to others.

To identify ways in which we can be kind to others.

✳ Activities:

1. Try to be kind

Talk with the children about the importance of kindness. Ask for a few examples of
people being kind.

In a round the children describe how someone was kind to them and then they say to
the person on their right "I am going to be kind to (the child's name) _____."

2. I was kind

In a round the children describe an act of kindness which they have shown to others.
Start with the phrase "I was kind to _____ when I _____".

For example "I was kind to my brother when I gave him one of my sweets".

3. Unkind

Discuss with the children feelings when people have been kind and unkind. Have any
children experienced unkind behaviour? How did they feel?

Relationships

6 years of
Circle Time

✳ Learning Objective:

To appreciate friends and the importance of friendship.

✳ Activities:

1. My friend

Talk with the children about the importance of friendship. Ask them to give some
    reasons for having friends.

In the circle each child in a round says two positive things about a friend of theirs.

For example: "My friend is a good runner and she cheers me up."

2. Helping my friend

Talk with the children about how we should help friends when they have a problem.
    Ask the children for examples of how we can help friends.

In a round each child gives one idea of how he/she can help a friend.

Use the statement: "I can be a friend by _____ _____".

Relationships

VALUING OTHERS YEAR 3

✱ Learning Objective:

To recognise and value the qualities of others.

✱ Activities:

1. I value you

Discuss with the children how they feel when someone says something to put them
down and when someone says something good about them.

Divide the children into pairs and each child questions the other to find something
good to say about their partner. In a round each partner makes two positive statements about each other.

For example, "Sue is good at netball. She has nice hair."

2. Thumbs up

Explain to the children that we can show we value others by what we say to or do to
them. Sometimes we can boost them up, other times we can put them down. In
the following brief story the children put their thumbs up when there is a "boost"
and thumbs down when there is a "put down".

Leena was late getting up. "You can never get up in the morning", shouted her
brother angrily. "I'm in the bathroom for the next 10 minutes anyway." "Hi,
Leena," says Mum, "I'll make you some breakfast while your brother gets ready."
Leena is ready to leave for school. "Have a good day", shouts Dad. "I'm sure you
will get that Maths right today".

When Leena arrives at school one of her friends says, "I like your new bag". In the
cloakroom someone pushes Leena out of the way and knocks her bag to the floor.
"Oh dear, new bag on the floor. Tough", the girl shouts and runs past.

In the classroom the teacher asks some questions. When Leena answers the teacher
says, "Well done, what a good try". One of the boys whispers "Swot! She thinks
she know everything".

At lunch time someone looks at Leena's sandwiches and says "Ugh - that looks like
cat food. You're not going to eat that, are you?" Leena's friend says, "Don't take
any notice. I think your food looks delicious."

Invite the children to describe other "thumbs up" and "thumbs down" experiences.

Relationships

✳ Learning Objective:

To practise being positive to other children in the class.

✳ Activities:

1. Aladdin's lamp

Divide the children into pairs. They talk about things that they would like to do to be better pupils and identify one for each child.

Then tell them that they have "pretend" magical powers. Bring out a "magic" object (e.g. a lamp, shell or metal container) which can be "rubbed". The one partner can wish for the other what is needed to be a better or happier pupil. For example, it might be that it involves improving handwriting. Therefore, the one child will say: "I wish that (name) will have better handwriting."

The children can talk about their wishes for others, e.g. family, friends, world-wide issues etc.

2. Sticky backs

Give each child a piece of paper. This is sellotaped on the back of the child to their right. Each child writes a positive comment about that child on her/his back.

In a round each child turns to the other person sitting next to her/him and that child reads out the comment.

An example of a positive comment might be: "Alex is a good writer."

✳ Resources:

"Magic" object.
Paper and sellotape.

Relationships

6 years of Circle Time

VALUING OTHERS   YEAR 5

✱ Learning Objective:

To explore feelings of worth and realise the important effect of feeling valued on others.

✱ Activities:

Explain to the group that we are going to discuss what it feels like to be valued.

These two simple exercises help children to explore the effect of positive statements.

1. You're good at _____

In a round each child turns to the one on his/her right and makes a positive statement about that child's ability, saying "Hello _____. I think you're good at _____."

For example, "Hello Peter. I think you're good at art".

After the round is completed ask the children to share their feelings. How did it feel to have someone compliment them in that way. What does it feel like to be valued?

2. I feel valued

Give each child a slip of paper with the sentence "I felt valued when _____". They complete the sentence and place the paper in a box.

The box is then passed around the circle and each child takes a piece of paper and reads it out to the group.

Ask the children to make any comments they wish about the statements. Were they surprised? How can they help other children to feel valued?

Relationships

6 years of **Circle Time**

✱ Learning Objectives:

To develop respect towards others.

To show encouragement towards others.

✱ Activities:

1. Respect me

Discuss with the group the meaning of the word "respect". Invite suggestions from the children.

The word "respect" has the idea of admiring someone because of certain qualities.

Produce some cards with the names of people who have done something worthy of people's respect. Divide the children into threes and give the cards to each group. Invite the children to discuss what the qualities are which might or might not, earn people's respect.

Examples of names (you might want to substitute the names of people you know the children have discussed previously): Mother Teresa; Ryan Giggs; Spice Girls; Princess Diana.

Go on to make the point that we all have some ability, skill or quality that will earn someone' respect. Ask the children to give some examples.

Children walk around the room and when teacher says STOP they have to shake hands with the person next to them and say "I respect you because _____."

2. The encouragers

Explain to the group that we all need encouragement to be able to cope with all that life demands from us. We are going to be "encouragers" today.

Invite the children to write on a small piece of paper something which they find difficult. It can be about school, home, friends etc. These are placed in a box and the box is passed around the circle. Each child takes one piece of paper and writes an encouraging comment underneath.

These are then placed back in the box. The box is passed around again and each child takes out one piece of paper and reads out the "difficulty" with the "encouragement".

Relationships

6 years of Circle Time

✱ Learning Objective:

To realise that we are all different and have different likes and dislikes.

✱ Activities:

1. Things I like

Talk with the children about how we are all different - we like different things and we dislike different things. Yet we need to get on together.

Choose different categories in which the children can say in a round what they like. For example, in the food category a child might say: "I like beans".

Examples of categories:

food; stories; TV programmes; books; games.

The exercise can be repeated using the categories to allow children to say what they do not like.

2. Change places

Talk with the children about the fact that we are all different with different likes and dislikes, but that we need to get on together. This game reminds us of that.

In the circle the teacher asks the children to stand up and change places if they like or dislike something. Make sure that the children understand that they have to be careful with one another as they move around the room. Choose a mixture of things which will produce a mixed response.

Examples might be: "Change places if you like....

toast; cabbage; chocolate; curry; ice-cream; having a bath; watching football; riding a bike; going to the dentist, etc.

✳ Learning Objectives:

To understand that friends sometimes disagree but can still be friends.

To identify ways in which friends who fall out can make up.

✳ Activities:

1. My good friend

In pairs the children discuss what they like about their friends. In a round each child gives an example of what they discussed. Begin with: "What I like about my friend is _____".

Then each pair discusses ways in which they have fallen out with friends. Invite the children to talk about their feelings when these things happen with a round beginning: "When I have an argument with my friend I feel _____".

2. Making up

In pairs children discuss ways in which friends sometimes disagree.

In a round they then give an example of this.

In the same pairs children discuss what they might do to make up a friendship and share this with the rest of the group.

Relationships

RESOLVING CONFLICT   YEAR 3

✱ Learning Objective:

To explore what makes us angry and likely to fall out with other children.

✱ Activities:

1. Angry

Raise with the children the fact that each one of us at some time gets angry. Sometimes that anger can get out of control and we lose our temper.

In a round the children say what has made them angry. The children use the phrase:
"Once I got angry when _____."

Focus on some of the examples the children gave in the round and discuss how they could deal with their feelings.

2. Cool down

Raise with the children the fact that each one of us at some time gets angry. Sometimes that anger can get out of control and we lose our temper.

Invite the children to talk about times when someone was angry with them and why this was so.

In a round ask each child to describe an occasion when someone (they should not name the person) was angry with them and how they responded. Use the phrase:
"Once someone was angry with me because _____. What I did was _____".

Focus on some of the examples the children gave in the round and discuss how they could have dealt with the anger shown.

Relationships

6 years of Circle Time

✳ Learning Objective:

To discuss examples of conflict and identify ways of resolving them.

✳ Activities:

1. Sorted

Talk with the children about the times we get into arguments and disagreements with other children. What are they about? Ask the children for examples and make a note of them.

Divide the children into pairs and give one of the suggested conflict situations to each pair. What solutions can they suggest which would resolve the conflict or make the situation better? Each pair shares in a round what they have decided.

2. "Okay" and "not okay"

Talk with the children about the times we get into arguments and disagreements with other children. We are going to discuss some common situations and suggest an "okay" response and "not okay" response.

Divide the class into threes and give each small group a card on which is written a conflict situation. The groups decide on the best way to talk about the conflict and feed back their responses in a round.

Examples to go on the cards:
- *Your friend lies to you*
- *Your friend says a lie about you to another child*
- *Another child calls you names*
- *Your brother and you both want to watch different television programmes*
- *Someone steals your pencil*
- *You and your sister at home both want to listen to different music*
- *Another child keeps hiding your bag*
- *Other children are making fun of you.*

Relationships

6 years of Circle Time

RESOLVING CONFLICT   YEAR 5

✱ Learning Objectives:

To develop an understanding of another person's point of view in
a conflict situation.

To use role-play as a means of putting oneself in another person's
shoes.

✱ Activities:

1. In your shoes

Explain to the children that when disagreements occur and conflict develops it is
important to try to understand what the other person is thinking or feeling. One
way of "getting into another person's shoes" is by role-play. The following scenarios are meant to be role-played by two children. If these are not appropriate
make up your own. If you wish, a third child can be an observer who can report
back on what took place.

It is important in a role-play that the roles are reversed so that both children have an
opportunity of experiencing each viewpoint.

*(a) You (the daughter/son) promised your friend that you would go swimming on Saturday
morning. You have really been looking forward to it.*

*(b) You (parent) need your daughter/son to help with the preparation for her little sister's
birthday party. You are annoyed that she has made other arrangements.*

(a) You like to play your stereo system loud. The music sounds better that way.

*(b) You are studying hard for your GCSEs and you need quiet. The music from the next room
is unbearable.*

*(a) You borrowed a tape from a friend, and you want to keep it longer. After all, your friend
has borrowed lots of things from you.*

*(b) You lent the tape to a friend. She has had it for three weeks and you want to listen to it. It
is your favourite tape.*

*(a) Your best friend is now ignoring you and spends time with someone else who lives around
the corner. You are upset about this. You feel rejected and let down.*

*(b) You don't spend any time with your friend now because he/she has been spreading rumours
about you and acting nastily. You don't want his/her company any more.*

Relationships

RESOLVING CONFLICT   YEAR 6

✱ Learning Objectives:

To develop the skills needed to deal with conflicts, especially
   bullying.

To practise some peer helping in resolving conflict.

✱ Activities:

1. LOC on (Listen - Options - Choice)

Discuss with the children the importance of being able to sort out disagreements and
   conflict before they become serious and even turn to violence.

Offer a framework for dealing with conflict which can be used by peer helpers working with the two children in conflict. Can they achieve a "win-win" situation.

- *Listen* - listen to the views and feelings of those involved in the conflict.
- *Options* - consider the options which might sort out the problem.
- *Choice* - choose the way forward (which is going to involve some give and take
       from both parties).

Divide the class into pairs and invite them to use the LOC framework for attempting
   a solution in the following scenarios. If these are not suitable make up your own.

*Matthew is being picked on by two other children and made fun of because he is tall for his
      age. He decides to get his own back by hiding their bags. They threaten to beat him up if
      he does not return the bags.*

*Linda is being left out of things by her friends. They say she is a snob and think she is above
      them. Linda is very upset and accuses them of bullying her by calling her names.*

*In a school football match Stephen accidentally fouls a member of the opposing team who lives
      in the same street as he does. The boy threatens to get his own back and gets some of his
      mates to hang around outside Stephen's house.*

*In the art lesson Rachel is messing around and accidentally spills some paint on Nicky's
      drawing. Rachel laughs and Nicky threatens to get her own back on some other work of
      Rachel's. Rachel tells her to grow up.*

Spiritual & Moral Development

Discussing sensitive issues
Solving problems
Reflection and meditation

Notes

✻ Learning Objective:

To discuss what we feel when we get hurt, and what we can do.

✻ Activities:

1. It hurt

Talk with the children about how sometimes other children can hurt us. When this happens we might cry and feel very upset.

In a round ask the children to describe an occasion when they were hurt by another child (but do not mention the name) and how they felt. Use the phrase "Once someone _____ and I felt _____".

Discuss with the children what they should do when another child hurts them.

2. Sticks and stones

Discuss with the children how sometimes we can be hurt not so much by someone hitting us, but by what they say. Give some examples

"No, you can't play with us"

"You've got funny coloured hair".

In a round ask the children to describe an occasion when they were hurt by what another child said (but do not mention the name) and how they felt. Use the phrase "Once someone said _____ and I felt _____".

Discuss with the children what they should do when another child hurts them in this way.

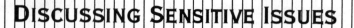

❋ Learning Objectives:

To understand the need to respect other children's property.
To develop empathy towards others who lose some property.
To discuss the importance of honesty.

❋ Activities:

1. Damaged

Start a discussion with the children about the things that are special to them and
   which would make them upset if they were damaged. Talk about how they might
   get damaged - it might be accidental or it might be the result of someone else's
   deliberate actions.

In a round each child talks about a time when something they valued was damaged,
   how it happened and how they felt. (No names should be mentioned!)

2. Stolen

Discuss with the children the fact that there is a lot of dishonesty in the world. Ask
   for some examples - people steal cars, steal clothes from shops, steal money etc.

Ask the children to think of how people must feel when someone steals something
   from them. Suggest some words - upset, angry etc.

In a round the children say what they would feel if someone stole their favourite toy,
   and why they think it is wrong to steal.

Spiritual and Moral

6 years of Circle Time

DISCUSSING SENSITIVE ISSUES YEAR 3

✱ Learning Objectives:

To recognise that bullying is not acceptable.

To develop the skill of empathy regarding bully and victim.

✱ Activities:

1. Bullying - zero tolerance

Talk to the children about what bullying is - someone deliberately hurting someone else over a period of time by what they say or do. Divide the class into pairs and ask them to think of examples of bullying they have seen or heard of (no mention of names).

In a round each child gives an example of bullying (using the words: "An example of bullying is _____") and make a zero tolerance statement, such as "this is not acceptable in this school".

For example, "An example of bullying is when someone keeps on calling someone else names, and this is not acceptable in this school".

2. Bullying - getting into their shoes

Talk with the children about "bullies" and "victims", i.e. those who hurt others and those who are hurt. What makes a bully do what he/she does, and what does the victim feel like? Ask for some ideas from the children.

In a round the children give their view about why they think children are bullies and what the feelings are of those who are bullied.

Use these sentences:

"I think a bully feels _____."

"I think someone who is bullied feels _____."

✱ Learning Objective:

To discuss situations that embarrass or worry us.

✱ Activities:

1. The Question

Read the poem entitled "The Question" to focus more directly on the worry of failure or failure itself in the school situation. For example able children might be frightened of attempting new difficult work in case of failure; some children are not satisfied unless everything is "perfect".

The Question

The child stands facing the teacher
(This happens every day);
A small embarrassed creature
Who can't think what to say.

He gazes up at the ceiling,
He stares down at the floor,
With a hot and flustered feeling
And a question he can't ignore.

He stands there like the stump of a tree
With a forest of arms around,
"It's easy, Sir, Ask me! Ask me!"
The answer, it seems, is found.

The child sits down with a lump in his throat
(This happens everywhere),
And brushes his eyes with the sleeve of his coat
And huddles in his chair.

by Allan Ahlberg (1991) "Heard it in the Playground" Puffin, Penguin Books Ltd.

Ask the children to write down other worries that they or their friends might have about school. Place them in a box and the teacher picks them out and asks for any suggestions that might help.

2. Oops!

Talk with the children about embarrassing moments. This should be a fun time! In a round the children talk about an embarrassing moment in their life.

Spiritual and Moral

DISCUSSING SENSITIVE ISSUES YEAR 5

❋ Learning Objective:

To develop understanding and consideration towards the feelings of children who are different in some way.

❋ Activities:

1. Different

Discuss with the children the fact that we are all different, and that some people are treated badly because of this. Read the poem and invite responses: (a) How did the child feel. (b) What other things are there about some children which cause them to be made fun of or left out?

A Boy without a name

I remember him clearly
And it was thirty years ago or more:
A boy without a name.

A friendless, silent boy,
His face blotched red, and flaking raw,
His expression, infinitely sad.

Some kind of eczema
It was, I now suppose,
The rusty, iron mask he wore.

But in those days we confidently swore
It was from playing near dustbins
And handling broken eggshells.

His hands, of course and knees
Were similarly scabbed, and cracked, and dry.
The rest of him we never saw.

They said it wasn't catching; still we knew
And strained away from him along the
corridor,
Sharing a ruler only under protest.

I remember the others; Brian Evans
Trevor Darby, Dorothy Cutler,
And the teachers; Mrs Palmer, Mr Waugh.

I remember Albert, who collected buttons,
And Amos, frothing his milk with a straw.
But his name, no, for it was never used.

I need a time-machine.
I must get back to nineteen fifty-four
And play with him, or talk, at least.

For now I often wake to see
His ordinary, haunting face, his flaw.
I hope his mother loved him.

Oh, children, don't be crueller than you
need.
The faces that you spit on or ignore
Will get you in the end.

by Allan Ahlberg (1991) "Heard it in the Playground"
Puffin, Penguin Books Ltd.

89

Spiritual and Moral

6 years of Circle Time

DISCUSSING SENSITIVE ISSUES | YEAR 6

✱ Learning Objective:

Developing awareness of drug related issues.

✱ Activities:

1. Drugtalk

Have a brainstorm on the word "drug". In a round the children say "When I think of the word "drug" I think of _____".

Establish that the word "drug" covers legal substances (e.g. paracetamol, alcohol, tobacco etc.) and illegal (e.g. ecstasy or cannabis).

Invite the children in a round to say why there is so much drug taking. Let the children use the phrase: "I think people take drugs because _____".

Use what they say to inform other sessions of drug education.

2. Don't just say no

Talk with the children about how sometimes people put pressure on us to do something. Ask for examples. Explain that it is important to say "no" if you feel that you are being put under pressure from a friend, but that it is also important to know why and say why you do not want to do something.

On pieces of card write some phrases that people might use about substances. Place them in a box and in a round each child takes one and adds a statement which is a challenge to the statement. For example, "It's cool to smoke .. but it's a real waste of money."

Examples of statements
- *It's cool to smoke _____ but _____ .*
- *You need alcohol to make a party go _____ but _____ .*
- *Paracetamol soon sorts out your headache _____ but _____ .*
- *Life is boring without drugs _____ but _____ .*
- *If you're in a disco you need something to keep you going _____ but _____ .*
- *People who don't drink are wimps _____ but _____ .*

90

Spiritual and Moral

SOLVING PROBLEMS   YEAR 1

❋ Learning Objectives:

To be able to identify who to go to with a worry.
To develop the confidence to share a worry.

❋ Activities:

1. My worry

Talk with the children about the fact that we all have worries. It is no good keeping
them inside us. We need to tell someone else who might be able to help us. Discuss the different people who the children might go to - Mum, Dad, brother,
sister, auntie, uncle, friend, cousin etc.

In a round the children use the phrase: "When I have a worry I tell it to _____".

2. Our worry

Talk with the children about the fact that we all have worries. It is no good keeping
them inside us. We need to tell someone else who might be able to help us. Sometimes we don't have the confidence to tell someone. Divide the children into
pairs. Each child tells the other what he/she is worried about using the phrase: "I
don't like _____."

Use the following categories: "I don't like going _____"
                                "I don't like doing _____"
                                "I don't like being _____".

In the circle invite any child to share the statements with the whole group.

✱ Learning Objectives:

To know where to go to find out information.
To work together to solve a problem.

✱ Activities:

1. Finding out

Talk with the children about the importance of knowing where to go to get information when trying to solve a problem.

Give the children some starter sentences. Here are some examples:

If I wanted to find out about dinosaurs I would go to the library.
If I wanted to find out about television programmes I would _____
If I wanted to find out about computers I would _____
If I wanted to find out about football I would _____
If I wanted to find out about going to the cinema I would _____ .

2. Two heads

Talk with the children about the fact that two heads are better than one in solving a problem.

Divide the class into pairs. Give each pair a card on which is written a problem to solve. Each pair feeds back their solution in the circle.

Examples of problems:

*   *You are hiding from your friends in the village hall. You are supposed to have gone home with your friend's mum. Then you realise that everyone has gone home and you are locked in.*

*   *You are in town with your mum or dad and you become separated. It is now ten minutes since you were together and you cannot see them anywhere.*

Spiritual and Moral

6 years of Circle Time

SOLVING PROBLEMS   YEAR 3

✱ Learning Objectives:

To work in a group to solve some dilemmas.
To discuss alternatives in solving a problem.

✱ Activities:

1. What would you do?

Divide the children into pairs and give each pair a card on which is written a dilemma
   to be discussed and a solution to be agreed.
In the circle one of the pair explains the dilemma and the other the solution they
   came up with.

Some examples of dilemmas:
- *You find a pound coin on the floor.*
- *You lose a toy that you borrowed from your friend.*
- *You see someone stealing in a shop.*
- *Your friend tells you that he/she is being bullied.*

2. Either - or

Divide the children into pairs and give each pair a card on which is written a problem.
   Each pair has to find two possible alternatives to solving the problem.
In the circle one of the pair explains the problem and the other the alternatives they
   came up with.
Examples of problems:
- *Your friend has a headache. What advice do you give? (Either _____ or _____)*
- *You fall and cut your knee. What do you do? (Either _____ or _____)*
- *You forget your dinner money. What do you do? (Either _____ or _____)*
- *Your friend says that she doesn't like you any more. (Either _____ or _____)*

✱ Learning Objectives:

To work together to solve problems.

To support others in the group who have problems.

✱ Activities:

1. Help!

Divide the children into pairs and give each pair a card on which is written a problem
to be discussed and a solution to be agreed.

In the circle one of the pair explains the problem and the other the solution they came
up with.

Examples of problems:

* *You have been asked to buy a present for your uncle but you do not know what he likes.*
* *You are playing the violin in the school concert and one of your strings snaps and you
haven't got a spare.*
* *You visit your grandmother and she has fallen down in the kitchen.*
* *Your friend wants you to go round his/her house. You don't want to and you say you are
not well. Your friend sees you out later with your parents.*

2. Listen to my problem

Explain to the children that the circle is an environment in which we support one
another. When we have problems we can help one another to work through
them.

Divide the children into pairs and each member of the pair shares with the other any
problem that they might have and any way in which they need help. The other
member tries to help by offering a way forward.

In the circle any child can share with the group a way in which he/she was helped by
his/her partner. <u>The problem does not have to be revealed.</u>

Alternatively, ask if any one has a problem they need help with. When that child
shares the problem the others are asked if they can help with a way forward.
When the "solutions" have been offered the child with the problem decides which
one could be of help.

Spiritual and Moral

6 years of **Circle Time**

✱ Learning Objective:

To develop negotiation skills as part of problem solving.

✱ Activities:

1. Win-win (personal)

Talk with the children about 'negotiation'. The word means trying to agree a solution that both people or sides are happy with. It is trying to achieve a 'win-win' situation as opposed to a 'win-lose' situation. In such negotiation both sides will have to give in to a certain extent, i.e. 'compromise'.

Divide the group into pairs and give out cards on which are written different situations which have caused a problem. The pair should try to come to a 'win-win' outcome by negotiating. The pairs then feed back in the circle their outcomes.

Examples of situations: (make up your own):

- *Your friend is offering to sell you a CD. You want it very much but the price is too high. Negotiate an agreement. Think carefully about the arguments you might use.*
- *You have agreed to go out with your friend. You want to go swimming; he/she wants to go to the cinema. Negotiate an agreement. Think about the arguments you might use.*
- *On the residential weekend there is only one place left and both of you want to go. Negotiate an agreement. Think carefully about the arguments you might use.*

2. Win-win (community)

Talk with the children about 'negotiation'. The word means trying to agree a solution that both people or sides are happy with. It is trying to achieve a 'win-win' situation as opposed to a 'win-lose' situation. In such negotiation both sides will have to give in to a certain extent, i.e. 'compromise'.

Divide into pairs and give out cards on which are written different conflict situations. The pair should try to come to a 'win-win' outcome by negotiating. The pairs then feed back in the circle their outcomes.

Examples of situations (make up your own):

- *The council wants to build a residential home for released prisoners. People living in the area protest that they will be at risk. Negotiate an agreement.*
- *Plans are being made to build houses on a park which is very popular with children and old people. Negotiate an agreement.*
- *An old house is going to be used as a hostel for people with alcohol problems. The local residents complain that there will be a lot of trouble in the area. Negotiate an agreement.*

✳ Learning Objective:

To attempt to solve problems using the PACE model.

✳ Activities:

1. Pace it (community)

Talk with the children about the way in which they solve problems. What are some of the ways in which you shouldn't solve a problem? e.g. tossing a coin, thinking of the first thing that comes into your head, doing unthinkingly what a friend suggests, panicking into an action, etc.

Suggest a simple model for problem solving. It consists of considering the possibilities for the solution, discussing the advantages and disadvantages of a possibility, making the choice and evaluating the action.

This the PACE model: Possibilities   Advantages   Choice   Evaluate

Divide the group into threes and give out cards on which are written different problems. Ask the children to use the PACE model in their discussion and feed back in the circle.

Examples of problems:

*   *Some children who want to skateboard have been banned from using the shopping precinct, but want to continue.*
*   *Nearby residents have complained about the noise from the disco in the youth club and are threatening to close down the youth centre.*

2. Pace it (global)

Suggest a simple model for problem solving. It consists of considering the possibilities for the solution, discussing the advantages and disadvantages of a possibility, making the choice and evaluating the action.

This the PACE model: Possibilities   Advantages   Choice   Evaluate

Divide the group into threes and give out cards on which are written different problems. Ask the children to use the PACE model in their discussion and feed back in the circle.

Examples of problems:

*   *The level of pollution from cars in the town centre is now dangerous. The shop keepers are worried that if cars are banned they will lose their trade.*
*   *There is a dramatic rise in violence by young people. Some say it is because of computer games and the police want these controlled.*

✻ Learning Objective:

To learn to be still and relaxed.

✻ Activities:

1. Relax!

The children sit on chairs in an upright position with their feet firmly on the ground. Younger children can sit on the carpet if there are squares or cushions for each space.

Ask the children to close their eyes and concentrate on their breathing. The slower the breathing the more relaxed they will feel.

Encourage the children to breathe in through the nose and out through the mouth. Breathe in slowly to the count of four and out to the same number.

2. All lit up

Ask the children to close their eyes and concentrate on their breathing. The slower the breathing the more relaxed they will feel.

Encourage the children to breathe in through the nose and out through the mouth. Breathe in slowly to the count of four and out to the same number

"Now imagine that there is a ball of light in front of you *(pause)*. What colour is the light? *(pause)*. You can feel the warmth of the light and now it is spreading through your body *(pause)*. Feel how warm and lovely it is *(pause)*. As it is spreading through your body you are feeling warm and peaceful and any bad feelings you have are going away. Now you are feeling peaceful, open your eyes and have a stretch."

✱ Learning Objective:

To learn to be still and relaxed and aware of one's feelings.

✱ Activities:

1. Candle meditation

Ask the children to close their eyes and concentrate on their breathing. The slower the breathing the more relaxed they will feel. Encourage the children to breathe in through the nose and out through the mouth. Breathe in slowly to the count of four and out to the same number.

Light a candle and place it in the middle of the circle.

With the room darkened if possible, let it flicker for a while. Ask the children to focus on the flame. Give more triggers for younger children - e.g. the flame flickering/dancing, the wax dripping/melting.

Move forward and blow out the candle, but keep still and quiet for a minute.

Ask the children what thoughts came to them as they watched the candle and what their feelings were.

2. Meditating on a present

Talk with the children about presents they have received. Have some been more special than others?

Use a stilling/breathing exercise to begin. See above for an example.

Place a nicely wrapped box in the middle of the room. Ask the children to look at it and think about some of the presents they have received. Play some quiet music as they think on this.

Ask the children in a round to tell everyone what presents they were thinking of, who gave it to them, and why it was special to them.

✱ Resources:

Candle.

Present, or some other object which you think is appropriate.

✱ Learning Objective:

To learn to be still and relaxed and aware of one's feelings.

✱ Activities:

1. In the country

Ask the children to close their eyes and concentrate on their breathing. The slower the breathing the more relaxed they will feel. Encourage the children to breathe in through the nose and out through the mouth. Breathe in slowly to the count of four and out to the same number.

Explain to the children that you are going to take them in their imagination to a lovely place that they will enjoy and that they can imagine again when they feel upset or worked up.

"Imagine that you are walking in the countryside along a peaceful country lane on a sunny summer's day. Ahead is an open gate and you walk through into a beautiful field (pause). What can you see? (pause). The grass is so green, there is a clump of trees and there is a mountain in the background. There are some birds singing in the trees. Listen to them (pause). As you walk along you come to a stream. The water is clean and fresh and you sit on the bank listening to the water splashing on the stones (pause). What can you hear? (pause). You reach down to place your hand in the water and splash it over your face to refresh you in the warm sun. You would like to stay here all day. But now you must come back to the classroom. Gently open your eyes and have a stretch."

2. A favourite toy

Use a breathing exercise as explained above to help the children relax.

Talk with the children about toys which they have at home. Which toy is especially dear to them? Place a toy in the centre of the room. Explain that you wish the children to concentrate their minds on the toy. Play some quiet music and then, leaving some appropriate gaps for the children to think, ask some questions about the toy. For example, where did it come from? *(pause)*. who do they think owned it? *(pause)*. how did the child who owned it play with it? *(pause)*. how precious was it to that child? *(pause)*. what things do we have which are precious to us and why?

✱ Learning Objectives:

To learn a strategy for relaxing.

To discuss ways of keeping calm in stressful situations.

✱ Activities:

1. Sit back and relax

Explain to the children that you are going to help them relax physically before going on to some reflective exercises.

Use this script for the exercise:

'You need to sit up straight, close your eyes, and concentrate on your breathing. Breathe in and out as slowly as possible. We are going to think of a number of different parts of the body and relax them. Let's start with the feet....pretend that you are digging your toes deeply into some sand....hold them tight in the sand (up to 10 seconds) and then let them go....feel how relaxed your feet are now. Next lift up your legs and stretch them out in front of you.....feel how tight the muscles are....hold them there and now place your feet back on the floor....feel how relaxed they are. Now focus on your back. Arch your back from the chair and hold it there (up to 10 seconds). Sit back in your chair and enjoy the feeling. We are now going to tighten the neck muscles....stretch your head back and hold....now let your head fall forward until it is floppy. Hold your hands out with the palms downwards....stretch your fingers upwards and hold them tight....now relax them. Your body should now feel quite relaxed....breathe in and out slowly....and relax any part of your body which still feels tense.

2. Stay cool

Talk with the children about the times that they get worked up or upset.

Divide the class into small groups and give each group three cards on each of which they will find a different situation. Ask each group to list three ways in which children react to the situations.

Examples of situations to write on the cards:

1. Parents shout and tell you off.   2. Your brother/sister breaks your toy.

3. You lose your pocket money.   4. You have a bad headache.

5. Someone picks on you.

What ways have you learned to help you to keep cool and relaxed?

✱ Learning Objective:

To use imagination to explore and reflect upon beauty.

✱ Activities:

Explain to the children that you want them to use their imagination to appreciate
   something wonderful and beautiful in nature.

The first visualisation is based on ideas from Mary Stone's "Don't Just Do Something
   - Sit There" (1992) published by RMEP. You can make up a similar visualisation
   using "stones".

1. Be a leaf

Bring some leaves into the classroom and give each child one which they then examine, Look at the colour, shape, markings. Feel texture, veins. Collect the leaves
   and then use a relaxation exercise followed by this script.

   *"Close your eyes gently now and imagine that you are the leaf which you have been looking at.
   You are on a branch on a tree in the park. You are quite safe and strongly attached to
   the branch. (pause). There is a gentle breeze and you can feel it cooling you in the warm
   sun (pause). You are swaying gently and rustling with the other leaves on the tree
   (pause). Soon it starts to rain - just a few spots at first and then a drizzle (pause). Feel
   the spots of water gently washing the dust off you and refreshing you (pause). After a
   few minutes the rain stops and you feel the sun drying the water on you and bringing
   warmth to the whole of you (pause). How are feeling now? (pause). Now we are going to
   return to the classroom. Gently open your eyes and have a stretch".*

In the circle invite the children to share their feelings and experiences.

2. Be a flower

Follow the procedure above.

   *"Close your eyes gently and imagine that you are a daffodil bulb. At the moment you are
   below the soil: it is dark and a little damp (pause). now something is happening - you
   are beginning to move in the soil and parts of you are sprouting (pause). in fact you are
   pushing up above the ground and becoming quite tall, although you cannot see anything
   yet (pause). what do you feel like now that you are above the ground? (pause). Now you
   are beginning to form a flower and feel yourself opening up (pause). you can see only a
   little at first and now more and more light is flooding into you, until you are completely
   open (pause). Feel the warmth of the sunshine and look at the colours around you."*

In the circle invite the children to share their feelings and experiences.

101

✳ Learning Objective:

To use imagination to explore and reflect upon sensitive issues.

✳ Activities:

Explain to the children that you want to take them into some imaginary situations in order that they can examine their feelings and decide what they should do. Start with a relaxation exercise and then use the scripts below.

1. A question of booze

"Close your eyes gently and imagine that you have been invited to a friend's party. Outside the house you can hear some music and when you go inside some of your friends are dancing and others are sitting around. The music is quite loud and you sit down for a while listening to all the sounds (pause). What can you hear? (pause). Who is making all the noise? (pause). Soon it is time for the food, and you are feeling hungry. In the next room the food is laid out on the tables and you help yourself (pause). What do you pile up on your plate? (pause). As you are eating one of your friends signals to you to come into the next room. When you get there three of your friends have got some alcoholic drinks, and they look a bit wobbly. They want you to join in (pause). what are you thinking? (pause). What do you say? (pause). Now gently open your eyes and have a stretch."

In the circle invite the children to share thoughts and intentions and discuss the issues which arise from making that choice. Talk about the risks and the consequences.

2. A question of forgiveness

"Close your eyes gently and imagine that you are living not long after the second world war. You had been imprisoned in a concentration camp in the war because you and your family had hidden away some Jewish people who were being rounded up by the Nazis. In the camp you had been treated very badly - you had been beaten, starved, made to work hard and your sister had died there (pause). Imagine the suffering of the prisoners, the cruelty of the guards, the illness and disease (pause). One day you were released. How did you feel? (pause). You believe there is a God who forgives even the most cruel person. One day you meet a former prison guard from the camp (pause). How do you feel towards him? (pause). He greets you and says that he wants you to forgive him for his cruelty. How do you react? (pause). What are your feelings? (pause). What do you do?

In the circle the children share their responses. Explore further the concept of forgiveness and how it can help future relationships.

The situation is based on an actual event in the story of Corrie Ten Boom (1976), The Hiding Place published by Hodder and Stoughton.

Bibliography

Ballard, J. (1982). Circlebook. Irvington.

Bliss, T. and Tetley, J. (1993).Circle Time. Lucky Duck Publishing.

Bliss, T. , Robinson, G. and Maines, B. (1995). Developing Circle Time. Lucky Duck Publishing.

Bliss, T. , Robinson, G. and Maines, B. (1995). Coming Round to Circle Time. (Video) Lucky Duck Publishing.

Curry, M. and Bromfield, C. (1994). Personal and Social Education in Primary Schools through Circle Time. Nasen.

Curry, M. and Bromfield, C. (1998). Circle Time, In-Service Training Manual. Nasen.

Mosley, J. (1991). All Round Success. Wiltshire County Council.

Mosley, J. (1993). Turn Your School Around. L.D.A.

Mosley, J. (1996). Quality Circle Time. L.D.A.

Robinson, G. and Maines. B. (1998).Circle Time Resources. Lucky Duck Publishing.

Timmerman, W. and Ballard, J. (1975). Strategies in Humanistic Education. Mandela.

White, M. (1991). Self Esteem: promoting positive practices for responsible behaviour. Circletime strategies for schools. Set A. Daniels.

White, M. (1992). Self Esteem: it's meaning and value in schools. Set B. Daniels.

White, M. (1999). Picture This. Lucky Duck Publishing.

Please note.
White. (1991) and White. (1992) are now published as one revised and combined publication, Magic Circles, building Self Esteem through Circle Time. Lucky Duck Publishing, (1999).

Notes